Beginner's Simple Step-by-Step Visual Guide

Make Your *first* QUILT
with Alex Anderson

1 Fun Block

12 Easy Layout Options

4 Sizes

C&T PUBLISHING

Text copyright © 2016 by Alex Anderson

Photography and artwork copyright © 2016 by C&T Publishing, Inc.

Publisher: Amy Marson

Creative Director: Gailen Runge

Editor: Liz Aneloski

Technical Editors: Del Walker and Debbie Rodgers

Cover Designer: Kristy Zacharias

Book Designer: Casey Dukes

Production Coordinator: Tim Manibusan

Production Editors: Jessica Brotman and Alice Mace Nakanishi

Illustrator: Kirstie L. Pettersen

Photo Assistant: Sarah Frost

Style photography by Page + Pixel and instructional photography by Diane Pedersen, unless otherwise noted

Published by C&T Publishing, Inc., P.O. Box 1456, Lafayette, CA 94549

Printed in China

10 9 8 7 6 5 4 3 2 1

Contents

Introduction

I love quilts. Are there any new quilters out there? The answer is yes—you!
I am often asked where a person interested in quilting should begin, so I
decided to write this book to get you, the beginning quilter, started with
the basics to make your first quilt. You must remember that there are many
different approaches to quiltmaking, and one is not better than the others,
just different.

A quilt is like a sandwich. It has three layers:

The quilt top is usually made of many 100% cotton fabrics that are cut
into pieces of various sizes and then sewn together either by hand or
by machine. This is called piecing.

The middle layer, called the batting, is usually either polyester or cotton.

The backing is another piece of 100% cotton fabric.

The three layers are then stitched together, joining the three components
(pieced top, batting, backing) into one. This is called quilting.

What this book provides is an introduction to the world of quiltmaking using
rotary cutting (as opposed to the templates that my grandma used), with
a simple wall quilt you can complete by making 16 of one basic, 12″ × 12″
finished quilt block and one additional block if you choose to add the border.
You will learn 3 basic techniques you will use over and over again in your
future quilting; strip piecing (four-patch units), quick half-square triangles, and
sew-and-flip construction (Flying Geese units). Fabric requirements are based
on standard 42″-wide fabric.

I recommend that you start with an easy, manageable project as your first quilt so you will be able to finish it and feel successful. I find that when first-time quilters start with a large project, the whole process becomes overwhelming, and they either give up in frustration or lose the enjoyment of the process. Besides, I want you to start with a manageable project so you can make another quilt sooner.

NOTE

ASSUMPTIONS

You know the following:

- How to use your sewing machine (This book is written for the new quilter, not the new sewist.)

- How to sew a straight line

- The basics of how to use a rotary cutter

I will teach you how to make one quilt block, so the fun of figuring out how to arrange the blocks and put the quilt together can begin sooner. Wait until you see how many options there are for arranging 16 of this one block!

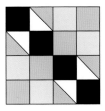

If you find that you really enjoy making this block, you can make more to complete a twin- or queen-size quilt (see the Appendix, page 44).

As you progress with your quilting, be sure to take classes. And be sure to check out your local quilting guild. You will meet great people there.

Quiltmaking is a journey both men and women have loved for generations. We all started at the same place, so there's no need to feel intimidated by a lack of experience.

My hope for you is that through making this quilt you will become familiar with a few of the basics of quiltmaking and develop into a quilt lover, as I have.

Alex Anderson, Quiltmaker

Tools

Quilters love gadgets, and every year more tools are introduced to the quiltmaking world. Your first visit to a quilt shop or the quilting section of a fabric store might be overwhelming. Many decisions need to be made when purchasing the necessary tools to get started quilting. The following shopping list provides the must-haves for anyone getting started. Many of the products come in different sizes. Please obtain the sizes recommended here. Later, you may want to add companion supplies, but the following are the best sizes to start with. Although the initial investment will seem costly, these tools will serve you for years if taken care of properly.

TOOLS AND SUPPLIES CHECKLIST

For more information, see Tools (page 6), Fabric (page 9), and The Basics (page 13).

- Rotary cutter
- Rotary cutting mat
- Rotary cutting ruler
- Scissors
- Pins
- Thread
- Seam ripper
- Iron
- Sewing machine

- Fabric
- Marking tools for quilting
- Batting
- Blue painter's tape (½" and 1" widths)
- Thread for hand sewing
- Needles for hand sewing
- Walking foot for machine quilting
- Safety pins for machine quilting basting

ROTARY CUTTER

This rolling razor blade mounted on a plastic handle is extremely dangerous and should be kept away from young children. I recommend the medium-size (45 mm) cutter.

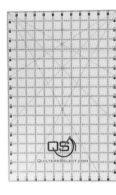

ROTARY CUTTING MAT

This self-healing plastic mat must be used in conjunction with the rotary cutter. I recommend either the medium or large mat. The medium one is great for starting out or for taking to a quilting class. The larger one is more versatile. Eventually you will want both sizes. Keep the mat out of direct sunlight and never leave it in a hot car, as the heat will cause the mat to warp and become unusable.

ROTARY CUTTING RULER

This tool was made especially for use with the rotary cutter and mat. It has ⅛" increments marked in both directions and is thick enough not to be cut by the rotary cutter. You will eventually have many rulers; to start with, I recommend a 6" × 12" rotary ruler. Remove the plastic wrap before using.

SCISSORS

Use 4"- to 5"-long shears with a sharp tip for clipping unwanted threads and fabric tips (bunny ears). Don't cut paper with fabric scissors, as doing so will quickly dull them.

PINS

Use fine glass-head pins. These are costly, but the less-expensive bargain brands are thick and will cause distortion when you are lining up seams. (I stock up when the good ones go on sale.)

THREAD

Use a quality cotton thread for piecing. Don't use decorative threads (such as metallic) or unusual fibers (such as rayon) for piecing. You can either match the thread color to your project or use a neutral gray or tan.

SEAM RIPPER

Yes, even the seasoned quilter uses a seam ripper. Splurge and get yourself a quality one (you'll know by the price). Cheap, dull rippers will cause the fabric to stretch and will create more problems than they are worth.

IRON

The one you have in your closet is probably just fine, but eventually you might want to purchase a super-hot steam iron. Correct pressing is very important in making a successful quilt.

SEWING MACHINE

Like cars, there are many different makes on the market. Eventually your sewing machine may be your biggest purchase, but for your first quilt you simply need one that is in good working condition, with proper tension; an even stitch; and a good, sharp size 80 needle.

That's it! The rest of the tools are gravy. If you are like most quilters, though, one day you will look into your sewing room and realize that the amount you paid for the contents could have put your firstborn through medical school. But shhh, don't tell anyone.

Fabric

Choosing Fabrics

Quilting stores, which are found all over the world, feature the finest 100% cotton fabrics available. Different grades of cloth are used for printed fabrics. You want to use the best you can find. The less-expensive cottons are loosely woven, with fewer threads per inch, and will only cause you problems as they stretch and distort. Stay away from poly/cotton blends, which will shrink right before your eyes as you press the shapes.

The fabric will dictate your quilt's mood or look.

NOTE

As I look back to my early days, I realize that I did not really start to feel confident with fabric choices until after I had made several quilts.

   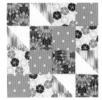

You will need one light-colored fabric, one dark-colored fabric, and three medium-colored fabrics for this quilt. Be sure the value (lightness or darkness) of your medium fabrics falls between the values of your light and dark fabrics.

NOTE

Value does the work and color gets the credit.

Once you have decided what look you want, there are two vital rules to keep in mind.

Always use light-, medium-, and dark-colored fabrics.

Use printed fabric that has variety in the character of the print. *Character of the print* refers to the design and scale (size) of the print on the cloth. Use fabrics with a range of small to larger designs on them. There are fabulous prints in delicious colors available to us.

Never judge a fabric by how it looks on the bolt. We are not making clothing. Remember, when the fabric is cut up, it will look quite different.

tip -

Try this trick: Take a 4″ square of cardboard and cut a 2″-square hole in the center. Position the cardboard over the fabric to see how the fabric will "read" when used in patchwork.

- -

Grain of the Fabric

When fabric is produced, threads are woven in two directions, creating what is called the straight of grain down the length and across the width. If you cut diagonally across the grain (in triangle pieces), you are working on the bias. Bias edges must be sewn and pressed carefully because they stretch easily. With this quilt, you will be piecing the triangles in a way that avoids any exposed bias edges. The long finished edges of the fabric are called the selvages. Always trim off the selvage edges—they can cause distortion of the block and are difficult to hand quilt through.

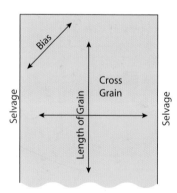

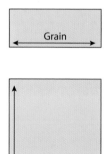

Preparing the Fabric

There are different schools of thought as to whether you should prewash your fabric. My philosophy is that you should, and here are three reasons.

When a quilt is made without prewashing the fabric, 100% cotton shrinks, causing puckers and distortion in the quilt.

Darker dyes have been known to migrate to lighter fabrics. This defines the term *heartbreak*.

Fabric is treated with chemicals, and I don't think it is healthy to breathe or handle these chemicals over an extended period. I sometimes find myself wheezing when I decide to pass up prewashing.

If you decide not to prewash, then at least test your fabrics. If you are working with dark pieces of fabric (reds and purples are extremely suspect), cut a 2″ square and put it in boiling water. If any color bleeds, wash your fabric in Retayne, Synthrapol, or a half-and-half solution of vinegar and water. Dry and retest the fabric. If it still runs, repeat the washing process. If the fabric continues to run, throw it away. It could ruin your quilt.

tips

Always prewash darks and lights separately.

When prewashing your fabric, unfold it completely before you put it in the washing machine so you don't get a permanent fade mark along the original fold.

Checklist
FOR MAKING A QUILT

1. Make the blocks.

DATE COMPLETED:

2. Sew the blocks together to create the quilt top.

DATE COMPLETED:

3. Cut and attach the borders.

DATE COMPLETED:

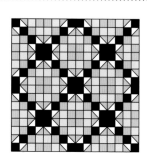

4. Layer the quilt top, batting, and backing.

DATE COMPLETED:

5. Safety-pin baste through all the layers.

DATE COMPLETED:

6. Machine quilt, attach the binding, and add a label.

DATE COMPLETED:

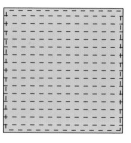
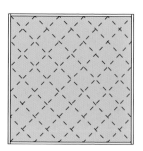

The Basics
Rotary Cutting

I love rotary cutting. Please practice this technique on some scrap fabric before starting on your project.

Cutting Strips

1. When rotary cutting strips of fabric, fold the fabric selvage to selvage and then fold again, bringing the first fold up to match the selvages. Line up the straight of grain as much as possible. This folding will give you 4 layers of fabric to cut through. Line up the edge of the fabric with the cutting mat's grid.

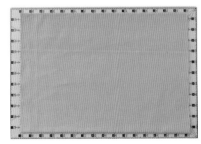

Fold fabric.

2. Position the fabric on the mat, keeping all sides of the fabric in line with the mat's grid. (To prevent the fabric from being pulled out of alignment, keep the fabric from hanging off the edge of the table.)

3. Line up the vertical marks on the ruler with the grid on the cutting mat. To square up the raw edges, place the ruler approximately ½" over the raw edges of the fabric. Be careful to position your hand so that none of your fingers are hanging over the side of the ruler where you will be cutting. Rest your pinkie finger on the outside edge of the ruler. This not only will help protect your finger but will also keep the ruler from moving.

4. Place the rotary cutter blade right next to the ruler. Depress the safety latch of the cutter, exposing the blade. Make a single pass (cutting away from your body) through the entire length of the fabric to remove the uneven raw edges.

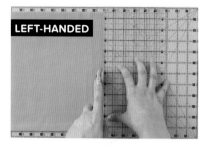

5. Move the ruler over 3½″ (to cut a 3½″ strip), lining up the vertical 3½″ mark on the ruler with the edge of the fabric. Line up a horizontal line on the ruler with a horizontal grid line on the mat and with the folded edge of the fabric. Cut the 3½″ strip. Practice this a few times to get the hang of it. Follow this same process to cut the strips needed for your quilting project.

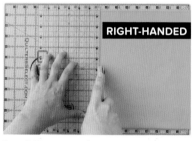

Step 4: Square up edge.

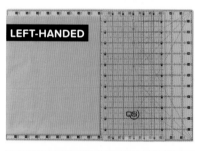

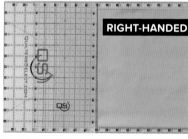

Step 5: Cut strip.

NOTES

- Rotary cutters are very sharp. Retract the rotary cutter blade after every cut. This is a good habit to develop from the start.

- If the strip you need to cut is wider than your ruler (6½″ border strips), use the grid lines on your rotary mat to help you cut the wide strip.

Cutting Squares and Rectangles

1. Place a 3½" strip so it is horizontal and parallel to one of the mat's grid lines. You can leave it folded and cut 4 squares or rectangles at a time (4 layers), or you can open the strip to cut 1 or 2 squares or rectangles at a time. Trim the edge of the fabric (Cutting Strips, Steps 3 and 4, page 13), but trim off only about ⅛" to square up the end of the strip.

2. Line up the vertical mark on the ruler that is the same as the width of the strip (in this case, 3½") with the edge of the fabric to cut a square (in this case 3½" × 3½"). Line up a horizontal line on the ruler with a horizontal grid line on the mat and with the folded edge of the fabric. Cut a square.

To cut rectangles, cut the strips to the length of the rectangle.

> **NOTES**
>
> ■ For the E squares in the project quilt, follow Cutting Strips (page 13).
>
> ■ For the half-square triangle units, follow Cutting Strips (page 13), except cut 3⅞"-wide strips.
>
> ■ For the Flying Geese blocks, follow Cutting Strips (page 13). Then follow Cutting Squares and Rectangles (above) to subcut the strips into 3½" × 3½" squares and 3½" × 6½" rectangles.

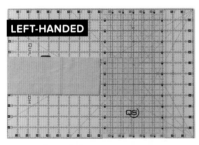

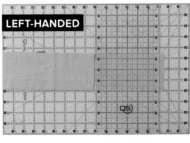

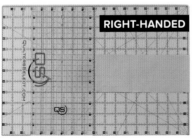

Cut square.

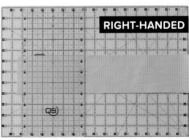

Cut rectangle.

Cutting Four-Patch Pieces

1. Referring to Four-Patch Units (page 31) in the project instructions, cut and sew the 2 strips together and press.

2. Position the 6½"-wide strip-pieced unit horizontal and parallel to one of the mat's grid lines. Trim the edge of the fabric (see Cutting Strips, Steps 3 and 4, page 13), but trim off only about ⅛" to square up the end of the strips.

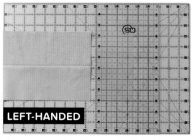

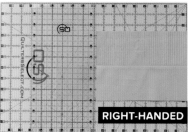

3. Line up the vertical 3½" mark on the ruler with the edge of the fabric to cut a 3½" piece. Line up a horizontal line on the ruler with a horizontal grid line on the mat and with the folded edge of the fabric. Cut a 3½" × 6½" piece.

Pinning

As you become acquainted with different quilters and quilting techniques, you will see that some people pin and some don't. I have found that the little time it takes to pin can determine the success of the block. Basically, you should pin where there are seams and intersections that need to line up or long edges that need to fit together.

Stitching

Set the stitch length on your machine just long enough so that your seam ripper slides nicely under the stitches. Backstitching is not necessary for this project because all the seam ends will be enclosed by other seams.

¼″ Seam Allowance

To piece the quilt top, you will always use a ¼″ seam allowance. The shapes in this book are all cut with the seam allowance included. Many machines have an exact ¼″ foot. If yours does, you are home free. If not, put your clear plastic rotary cutting ruler under the sewing machine needle, drop the presser foot, and then manually ease the needle down on top of the ¼″ mark. Take a thin piece of masking tape and mark the ¼″ measurement on the throat plate, using the edge of the ruler as your guide.

As you sew the pieces together, use this piece of tape as your seam guide. This is an extremely important step for ensuring accuracy. Take the time to understand your machine's ¼″. My kids' term *close enough* will only reward you with yards of frustration.

1½″

tip –

To check your ¼″, Sally Collins of Walnut Creek, California, recommends that you cut 2 strips of fabric each 1″ × 3½″. Sew the 2 strips together along one 3½″ side, press, and measure. The sewn unit should be 1½″ wide. If not, try again until you find your machine's perfect ¼″.

Seam Ripping

On occasion, you will need to pick out a seam. Cut every third stitch on one side of the fabric; then lift the thread off the other side of the fabric.

Pressing

Pressing is a very important component of quiltmaking. Many beginners approach the pressing portion of quiltmaking as if they were ironing the weekly laundry. Old habits are hard to break, but you must learn this new technique if you want to have super-looking quilts. The following tips are for pieced units.

Press on a firm surface (an ironing board with a single pad). Seams are usually pressed in either one direction or the other (not open). Press in the direction indicated by the arrows in the instructions—first on the wrong side, then on the right side. This helps the seams align in your block construction and prevents tucks from being pressed into the sewn seams.

Setting Options

The arrangement of blocks for this quilt is called a straight set. This means that the blocks are positioned with the sides vertical and horizontal to the quilt's edges.

This wonderful block gives you lots of setting possibilities. After you have made the 16 blocks, use the setting shown in the project instructions or choose your favorite setting from the options that follow.

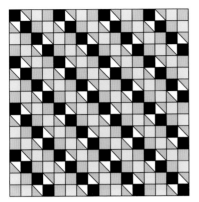

Setting 1

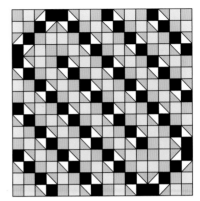

Setting 2

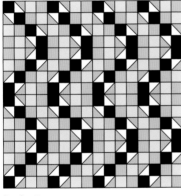

Setting 3

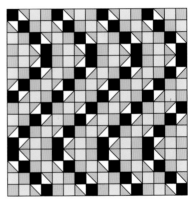

Setting 4

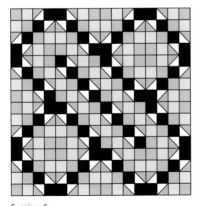

Setting 5

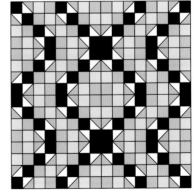

Setting 6

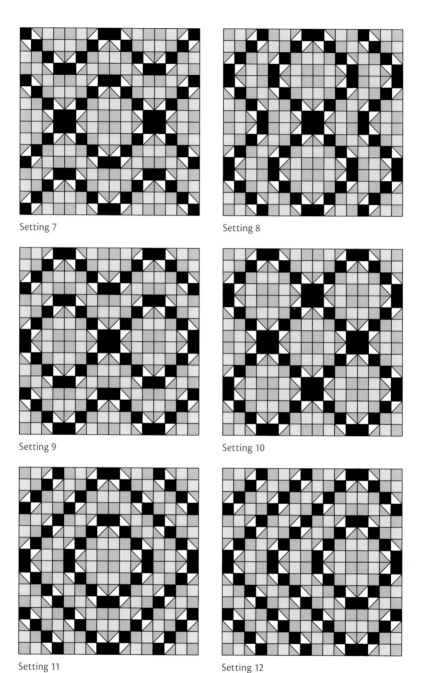

Setting 7

Setting 8

Setting 9

Setting 10

Setting 11

Setting 12

The Quilt Sandwich

Backing

Choosing the fabrics for the backing can be as much fun as deciding on the fabrics for the front of the quilt. It's okay to use a variety of fabrics for one backing.

Here are a few things to keep in mind:

Always prewash and cut off the selvage edges before piecing the fabric together. It is difficult to hand quilt through the selvages, and the seams won't lie flat.

If your quilt top has a lot of white in it, use light colors for the backing so the colors don't show through the batting to the front.

Always make the backing a few inches larger than the quilt top, on all four sides, in case your quilt top shifts during quilting.

Never use a sheet or a piece of decorator fabric for the backing. This fabric has a high thread count and is difficult to hand quilt.

Batting

The batting should be a few inches larger than the quilt top on all four sides.

For machine quilting, I recommend that you use 100% cotton batting. Make sure you follow the instructions on the package and prewash if necessary.

Layering

Depending on the size of my project, I work either on a tabletop (small quilt) or on my nonloop carpet (large quilt). First, place the quilt backing on your work area, wrong side up. Either tape it down (tabletop) or pin using T-pins (carpet), working from the center of each side to the corners. Keep the fabric grain straight and make sure the backing is stretched taut. No bubbles or ripples are acceptable; otherwise, you will have folds and tucks in the back of your finished quilt.

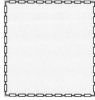

Tape backing.

Carefully unroll the batting and smooth it on top of the backing. Trim the batting to the same size as the backing. Smooth the quilt top onto the batting, right side up. The quilt top should be a few inches smaller than the backing and batting on all four sides.

Basting for Machine Quilting

The purpose of basting is to hold the layers together and prevent them from shifting during quilting. The basting will be removed when the quilting is finished.

Pin baste with safety pins every 3" across the quilt and around the edge. Pin evenly across the quilt.

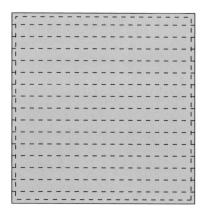

tip - - - - - - - - - - - -

Special safety pins are available for quilt basting. You can purchase packages of nonrusting pins that are all the same size; some brands are curved for easier pinning.

Machine Quilting

Quilting is the act of stitching the three layers together.

For your first project, I recommend that you keep the quilting as simple as possible. Start by quilting-in-the-ditch. This is done by quilting as close as possible to the sewn seam on the side without the seam allowance. It is a great way for a beginner to start. Your stitches will be hidden, giving you time to perfect your quilting technique. I also love using a simple grid that covers the entire surface of the quilt.

Marking Tools

There are many options for marking your quilt top. For straight-line quilting, I usually use a Verithin pencil, a white chalk pencil, or painter's tape. The chalk comes off easily and the tape is easily removable. Both options are great! Never use a regular graphite pencil, because it may not come out (especially after pressing).

Before marking the quilt top, always test the marking tool on your fabric first to make sure the marks come out.

Marking a Basic Grid for Machine Quilting

Mark diagonal lines as shown or place painter's tape diagonally through the corners of the block pieces in one direction. After you have stitched these diagonal lines, remove the tape and place tape diagonally in the other direction.

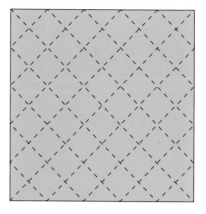

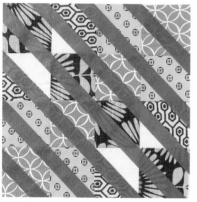

Tape diagonally in one direction.

After stitching, place tape diagonally in other direction.

Machine Quilting Supplies

Machine quilting is an art form of its own. With practice, machine quilting can be a beautiful addition to your quilts.

You will need:

WALKING FOOT

When you quilt using a sewing machine, the layers of fabric and batting may not feed in evenly. Depending on your sewing machine, it can be very difficult to machine quilt without getting tucks in the backing. A walking foot helps solve this problem; it feeds the layers of fabric evenly through the sewing machine.

> **NOTE**
>
> If you don't have a separate or built-in walking foot for your sewing machine and don't want to purchase one, consider having your quilt quilted by one of the many professional quilters who do this for a living.

THREAD

Use 100% cotton thread in a color that blends with the quilt top (usually a medium color).

Machine Quilting Needles

I use a topstitch 80. It's good for all-purpose machine quilting.

Machine Quilting Stitches

Support your quilt on all sides. Quilt on a large table. You can use an ironing board, adjusted to your table height, on the left-hand side and perpendicular to the table. Ideally, your sewing machine should be recessed into the table to create a level surface, but this is not absolutely essential.

1. To start machine quilting, reduce your stitch length almost (but not exactly) to 0 and lower the presser foot right over the spot where you plan to start quilting. Holding on to the top thread, take a complete stitch, so the needle returns to its highest position.

2. While raising the presser foot, gently tug the top thread to pull the loop of bobbin thread to the quilt surface. Pull the end of the bobbin thread through to the top.

Step 1: Take 1 complete stitch, ending with needle at its highest position.

Step 2: Pull top thread to bring loop of bobbin thread to surface.

3. Insert the needle into the exact spot where the bobbin thread came up. Hold the threads to the side as you take 1 or 2 stitches.

4. Gradually increase the stitch length (to approximately 10–12 stitches per inch) over 6–8 stitches and continue to stitch the row. When you're ready to end a row of stitching, gradually decrease the stitch length back to almost 0 and stitch a few more stitches.

5. Stitch-in-the-ditch between the blocks, a row in each direction (closest to the center), both vertically and horizontally, to secure the 3 layers. Then work from the center out as you stitch-in-the-ditch the remaining lines. After the center quilting is complete, stitch-in-the-ditch on the border seams.

6. Stitch the marked grid to complete your machine quilting.

Step 3: Insert needle and take 1 or 2 stitches.

Step 4

Crossroads
PROJECT INSTRUCTIONS

Quilted by Dianne Schweickert

You may choose to make this quilt with or without borders.
See the Appendix (page 44) for more quilt size options.

- **Finished quilt block:** 12″ × 12″
- **Number of blocks:** 16
- **Finished quilt with optional borders:** 65½″ × 65½″
- **Finished inner border width:** 2½″
- **Finished outer border width:** 6″
- **Finished Flying Geese border block:** 6″ × 12″
- **Number of Flying Geese outer border blocks:** 4
- **Finished quilt without borders:** 48″ × 48″ (plus binding)

NOTES

- The term *finished* means that this is the size after the piece has been sewn into the quilt. This size no longer includes the seam allowances. Thus, a 12½″ × 12½″ block becomes 12″ × 12″ finished once it has been sewn into the quilt.

- You can choose to make this quilt with or without borders.

FABRIC REQUIREMENTS

Fabric requirements are based on 42" fabric width.

Fabric A (medium-colored orange print)
¾ yard for main blocks

Fabric B (medium-colored green print)
¾ yard for main blocks

Fabric C (medium-colored blue print)
⅝ yard for main blocks and ⅜ yard for background of Flying Geese outer border blocks (optional)

Fabric D (white)
⅝ yard for main blocks, ½ yard for inner border (optional), and ⅜ yard for triangles of Flying Geese outer border blocks (optional)

Fabric E (dark multicolored print)
¾ yard for main blocks and 1⅜ yards for outer border (optional)

NOTE

If your outer border fabric is a lengthwise directional print, purchase enough fabric to cut the outer border strips (see Outer Border, page 37) from the length of the fabric (parallel to the selvages). You will need to cut all the strips so that the area of the printed design matches in all the strips.

tip - - - - - - - - -

If you choose a backing fabric that will also work as the binding, you can use the extra backing fabric for the binding and not purchase separate binding fabric.

- - - - - - - - - - - - -

Backing
3 yards without borders or 4 yards with borders

Batting
52" × 52" without borders or 70" × 70" with borders

Binding
⅜ yard without borders or ½ yard with borders

NOTE
IMPORTANT REMINDERS

- Be sure to read the chapters Tools (page 6), Fabric (page 9), and The Basics (page 13) before beginning. *No, really. Read these chapters first. You will learn important information to make your quilting experience more successful.*

- It is very important to use an exact ¼" seam allowance (page 17) to make your blocks accurate.

Make 16.

Arkansas Crossroads Blocks

Use ¼" seam allowance.

Four-Patch Units

PIECING AND PRESSING

CUTTING ✂

**Fabric A
(orange print)**
Cut 6 strips
3½" × width of fabric.

**Fabric B
(green print)**
Cut 6 strips
3½" × width of fabric.

1. Sew together the Fabric A and Fabric B strips into 6 pairs (strip sets), pinning as necessary. Press, following the arrows. Each strip set should measure 6½" wide.

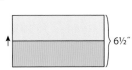

2. Cut these strip sets into 64 pieces 3½" wide. (You will get about 11 pieces per sewn strip.)

3. Pin together 2 pieces, as shown below, matching the center seams.

PINNING

When aligning seams that are pressed in opposite directions (as in this four-patch unit), place pins on both sides of the seam, no more than ⅛" from each side.

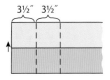

---

4. Sew together the pieces in pairs to make 32 four-patch units, pinning as necessary. Press, following the arrows.

Half-Square Triangle Units

CUTTING

**Fabric C
(blue print)**

Cut 4 strips
3⅞" × width of fabric;
subcut into
32 squares 3⅞" × 3⅞".

**Fabric D
(white)**

Cut 4 strips
3⅞" × width of fabric;
subcut into
32 squares 3⅞" × 3⅞".

PIECING AND PRESSING

1. Lay a Fabric D square on top of a Fabric C square with right sides together.

2. Draw a line from corner to corner with a pencil on the Fabric D square.

3. Draw a line ¼" from each side of the first line.

4. Stitch on the outer drawn lines, pinning as necessary.

Sew.

5. Trim on the first drawn line.

6. Press open, following the arrow.

7. Repeat Steps 1–6 to make 64 half-square triangle C/D units.

Constructing the Blocks

CUTTING

Fabric E
(multicolored print)
Cut 6 strips
3½" × width of fabric;
subcut into
64 squares 3½" × 3½".

1. Lay out a half-square triangle C/D unit with a Fabric E square as shown.

2. Place the half-square triangle C/D unit on top of the Fabric E square, with right sides together, and stitch as shown, pinning as necessary.

Half-square triangle unit
C/D on top of E square.

Open the pieces and make sure the half-square triangle unit is positioned as shown above.

3. Press, following the arrow.

4. Repeat Steps 1–3 to make 64 C/D/E units.

5. Lay out 2 of the C/D/E units as shown.

6. Place 1 C/D/E unit on top of the other C/D/E unit, right sides together. Match the center seams, pin as necessary, and stitch.

Stitch 2 C/D/E units together.

Open the pieces and make sure the units are positioned as shown.

7. Press, following the arrow.

8. Lay out a half-square triangle C/D/E unit with a four-patch unit as shown.

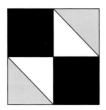 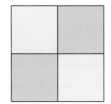

9. Place the four-patch unit on top of the half-square triangle C/D/E unit, right sides together. Match the center seams, pin as necessary, and stitch.

 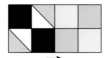

Stitch four-patch unit
to C/D/E unit.

Open the pieces and make sure the units are positioned as shown above.

10. Press, following the arrow.

11. Repeat Steps 5–10 to make 32 half-blocks.

12. Lay out 2 of the half-blocks as shown.

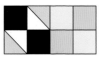
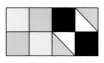

Step 12

13. Place 1 half-block on top of another half-block, right sides together. Pin together, matching the seams, and stitch.

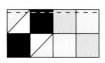

Step 13

Open the pieces and make sure the units are positioned as shown.

14. Press, following the arrow.

15. Repeat Steps 12–14 to make 16 blocks.

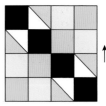

Step 13

Choosing a Setting

1. Arrange the blocks as shown below, choose one of the other setting options (pages 19 and 20), or come up with your own arrangement.

(pages 19 and 20)

Try several options by laying out your blocks to see which one you like best. Take a photo of each setting you try, so you can compare the photos and choose your favorite.

Quilt Top Construction

1. Lay out the blocks in your favorite setting. If you use the same one I did, it will look like this (at right).

2. Sew the blocks into rows, pinning as necessary, and press, following the arrows.

3. Sew the rows together, matching the seams and pinning as necessary. Press, following the arrows.

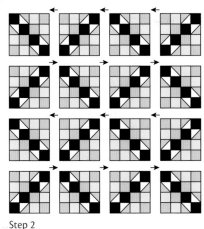

Step 2

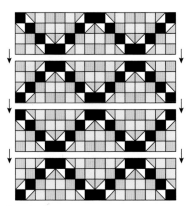

Step 3

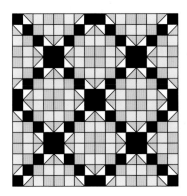

Borders (optional)
Inner Border

1. For the top and bottom inner borders, cut
3 strips 3″ × width of fabric from Fabric D (white).

2. Trim off the selvages and sew together end to
end into 1 long length for the top and bottom
inner borders.

3. Measure your quilt top across the center from
side to side.

4. Cut the top and bottom inner border strips this
length from the long length of inner border fabric
prepared in Step 1. Save the leftover strip for the
side inner borders.

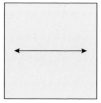

Step 3

5. Find the center of the quilt top and the center
of the top inner border strip by folding them
in half and pinning them together, right sides
together. Pin the ends of the inner border strip to
the corners of the quilt top and then pin every 2″.

6. Sew and press, following the pressing arrows.

Step 6

7. Repeat Steps 4 and 5 for the bottom border.

8. For the side inner borders, cut 2 strips
3″ × width of fabric from Fabric D (white).

9. Trim off the selvages and sew together end to
end into 1 long length for the side inner borders,
adding the leftover strip from the top and bottom
inner borders.

Step 7

10. Measure your quilt top from top to bottom
across the center, including the top and bottom
borders.

11. Cut the side inner border strips to this length.

12. Find the center of a side of the quilt top and the center of a side inner border strip by folding them in half and pinning them together, right sides together. Pin the ends of the inner border strip to the corners of the quilt top and then pin every 2".

13. Sew and press, following the pressing arrows.

14. Repeat Steps 12 and 13 for the other side inner border.

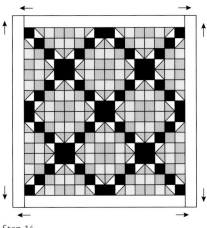

Step 14

Outer Border
FLYING GEESE BLOCKS

CUTTING

Fabric C (blue print)
Cut 3 strips 3½" × width of fabric; subcut into 32 squares 3½" × 3½".

Fabric D (white)
Cut 3 strips 3½" × width of fabric; subcut into 16 rectangles 3½" × 6½".

1. Draw a line from corner to corner on the wrong sides of 2 Fabric C squares.

2. Place a Fabric C square on a corner of a Fabric D rectangle. Be sure to match the direction of the drawn line as shown.

3. Stitch on the line, pinning as necessary.

4. Trim, leaving a ¼" seam allowance as shown.

NOTE

If you are using a directional print, cut the following strips lengthwise (parallel to the selvages) rather than across the width of the fabric (selvage to selvage). This will give you strips with the fabric design running all the same direction when you add the border strips to the quilt top.

---

5. Press, following the arrow.

6. Place the other Fabric C square on the other corner of the Fabric D rectangle. Be sure to match the direction of the drawn line as shown.

Step 5

7. Stitch on the line, pinning as necessary.

8. Trim, leaving a ¼" seam allowance as shown.

Step 7

9. Press, following the arrows.

10. Repeat Steps 1–9 to make 16 Flying Geese units.

Step 9

11. Lay out 4 of the Flying Geese units.

12. Sew pairs of the Flying Geese units together, right sides together, with the piece requiring the exact point on top, pinning as necessary.

Step 12: Place 1 Flying Geese unit on top of another Flying Geese unit.

13. Press, following the arrows.

Step 11

14. Lay out the pairs of Flying Geese units.

15. Sew the pairs together.

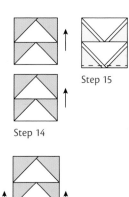

Step 15

16. Press, following the arrows.

17. Repeat Steps 11–16 to make 4 Flying Geese blocks.

Step 14

Step 16

CUTTING

**Fabric E
(multicolored print)**
Cut 4 strips
6½" × width of fabric
and trim off the selvages.

Cut 2 strips
6½" × width of fabric;
subcut each strip into
1 rectangle 6½" × 12½"
and 1 rectangle 6½" × 18½".

*You will have 2 rectangles
6½" × 12½" (for top and
bottom outer borders) and
2 rectangles 6½" × 18½"
(for side borders).*

OUTER BORDER STRIPS

1. Sew a 6½" × 12½" Fabric E strip to a Flying Geese block as shown. Make 2.

2. Sew a full strip of Fabric E to the other end of the Flying Geese block. Make 2.

3. Measure your quilt top across the center from side to side.

4. Trim off the long ends of Fabric E from the Step 2 strips so the top and bottom outer borders measure this length.

5. Find the center of the quilt top and the center of the top outer border strip by folding them in half and pinning them together, right sides together. Pin the ends of the outer border strip to the corners of the quilt top and then pin every 2".

Step 1   Step 2

6. Sew and press, following the pressing arrows.

7. Repeat Steps 5 and 6 for the bottom border.

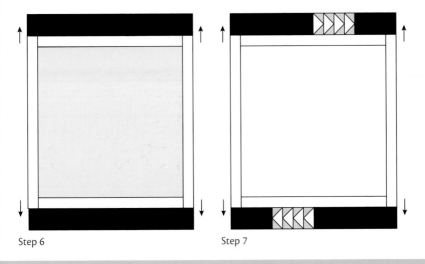

Step 6   Step 7

8. Sew a 6½" × 18½" Fabric E strip to a remaining Flying Geese block as shown. Press in the direction of the arrows. Make 2.

9. Sew a full strip of Fabric E to the other end of the Flying Geese block. Press in the direction of the arrows. Make 2.

10. Measure your quilt top from top to bottom across the center, including the borders.

11. Trim off the long ends of Fabric E so the outer borders measure this length.

12. Find the center of a side of the quilt top and the center of a trimmed side outer border strip by folding them in half and pinning them together, right sides together. Pin the ends of the outer border strip to the corners of the quilt top and then pin every 2".

13. Sew and press, following the pressing arrows.

14. Repeat Steps 12 and 13 for the other side outer border.

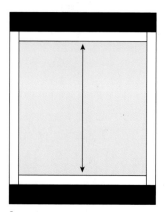

Step 8 Step 9

Step 10

Step 13

Finishing Your Quilt
Layering and Quilting

Because the project quilt is wider than the standard 42" fabric width, you will need to piece the backing to make it wide enough.

1. Cut the backing fabric in half, selvage to selvage, and trim off the selvages.

2. Sew the 2 secwtions of the backing fabric together along the long edges to create a piece of fabric wide enough to cover the quilt top. Press the seam open.

3. Layer the backing (wrong side up), with the batting on top, aligning a corner of the batting on top of the backing. Trim the backing to the size of the batting. This will make the best use of your fabric and give you the largest leftover piece for the binding or a future project. See Backing (page 21), Batting (page 21), and Layering (page 22).

4. Place the quilt top on the batting (right side up), centering it within the square of the batting.

5. Baste the layers (see Basting for Machine Quilting, page 22).

6. Machine quilt a simple grid (see Machine Quilting Stitches, page 26).

7. Trim the batting and backing even with the edges of the quilt top.

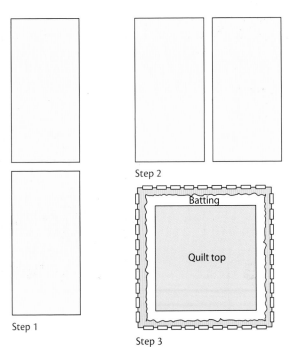

Step 1

Step 2

Batting

Quilt top

Step 3

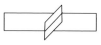
Cut 5 strips
2¼" × fabric width
(for quilt without borders).

Cut 7 strips
2¼" × fabric width
(for quilt with borders).

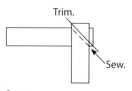

Step 1

Step 2

Step 3

Binding

The binding covers the edges of the three layers and often gets the most abuse when a quilt is loved and used.

1. Piece the strips together into a single long length with angled seams, as shown, to prevent big lumps in the binding. Trim ¼" away from the seam.

2. Press the seams open.

3. Fold and press lengthwise.

4. Measure your quilt across the center from side to side.

5. Trim the top and bottom binding strips to this length plus 1".

6. On the top edge of the front of the quilt, line up the raw edges of the binding with the raw edge of the quilt. Let the binding extend ½" past the corners of the quilt. Sew using a ¼" seam allowance.

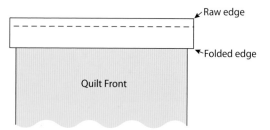

7. Repeat for the bottom edge of the quilt.

8. Flip the finished edge of the binding over the raw edge of the quilt and slipstitch the binding to the back of the quilt. Trim the ends even with the edges of the quilt, as shown.

9. Measure your quilt across the center from top to bottom.

10. Trim the strips to this measurement plus 1″ for turning under.

11. On a side edge of the front of the quilt, line up the raw edges of the binding with the raw edge of the quilt. Let the binding extend ½″ past the corner of the quilt on each side. Sew using a ¼″ seam allowance.

12. Repeat for the other side edge.

13. Fold over the short ends of the binding to create a finished edge; then fold the binding to the back of the quilt. Hand stitch in place.

14. Always sign, date, and document your project on the quilt backing with a permanent marking pen designed specifically for fabric.

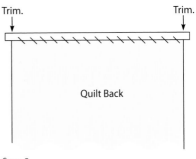

Trim. Trim.

Quilt Back

Step 8

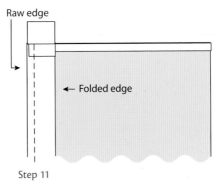

Raw edge

← Folded edge

Step 11

Fold.

Quilt Back

Step 13

Appendix

The charts on the following pages will give you the yardage requirements and cutting instructions for twin-, and queen-size comforter-style quilts without borders. Measure your mattress and compare it to the finished quilt measurements to be sure the sizes given here will work for your mattress.

STANDARD MATTRESS AND QUILT SIZES

All measurements reflect finished sizes (page 29).

STANDARD MATTRESS SIZE		COMFORTER* (12″ BLOCKS)	COVERLET** (12″ BLOCKS)	BEDSPREAD*** (12″ BLOCKS)
Twin	39″ × 75″	66″ × 90″	72″ × 102″	78″ × 108″
Full	54″ × 75″	78″ × 90″	84″ × 102″	96″ × 108″
Queen	60″ × 80″	88″ × 94″	94″ × 106″	100″ × 112″
King	78″ × 80″	106″ × 94″	112″ × 106″	118″ × 112″

* *Comforters cover the mattress but not the box spring; no pillow tuck.*
** *Coverlets cover the mattress and box spring and have a pillow tuck.*
*** *Bedspreads cover the bed almost to the floor and have a pillow tuck.*

Twin- and Queen-Size Options

Use the charts that follow, along with The Basics (page 13) and the project instructions (page 28), to make a twin- or queen-size comforter-style quilt.

Twin: 72" × 96"; 48 blocks; 6 × 8 block layout
Queen: 96" × 96"; 64 blocks; 8 × 8 block layout

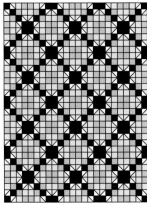

Twin size

Queen size

FABRIC REQUIREMENTS

Fabric requirements are based on 42" fabric width.

FABRIC	TWIN	QUEEN
Fabric A (orange print)	1⅞ yards	2½ yards
Fabric B (green print)	1⅞ yards	2½ yards
Fabric C (blue print)	1¼ yards	1⅝ yards
Fabric D (white)	1¼ yards	1⅝ yards
Fabric E (multicolored print)	2⅜ yards	2½ yards
Backing	76" × 100"	100" × 100"
Batting	76" × 100"	100" × 100"
Binding	⅝ yard; 9 strips 2¼" × fabric width	¾ yard; 10 strips 2¼" × fabric width

CUTTING

Fabric	TWIN		QUEEN	
	Number of 3½"-wide strips	Number of 3½" subcut squares	Number of 3½"-wide strips	Number of 3½" subcut squares
Fabric A (orange print)	18	n/a	24	n/a
Fabric B (green print)	18	n/a	24	n/a
Fabric E (multi-colored print)	18	192	24	128
	Number of 3⅞"-wide strips	Number of 3⅞" subcut squares	Number of 3⅞"-wide strips	Number of 3⅞" subcut squares
Fabric C (blue print)	10	96	13	128
Fabric D (white)	10	96	13	128

NUMBER OF ELEMENTS

	TWIN	QUEEN
Four-patch units	96	128
Half-square triangle units	192	256

About the Author

Alex Anderson's love of quilting began in 1978 when she completed a Grandmother's Flower Garden quilt as part of her work toward a degree in art from San Francisco State University. She has an intense appreciation of traditional quilts and beautiful quilting surface design.

She is the author of 30 books in four languages selling more than 1 million copies worldwide. She is the national spokesperson for BERNINA of America, Inc. as well as a designer with RJR Fabrics, MasterPiece Thread (Superior Threads), and Quilters Select (Floriani).

Alex is a founding partner of TheQuiltShow.com with Ricky Tims. *The Quilt Show* is the world's first full-service interactive online video/web TV show created just for quilters worldwide. With more than 140,000 registered members in more than 100 countries, the show aims to educate, inspire, entertain, connect, and grow the world quilting community in a fun, positive, and interactive environment.

Alex received the International Quilt Festival's 2008 Silver Star Award, an award given annually to a recipient *"whose work and influence has made—and continues to make—a sizable and positive impact on the quilting industry and community."*

Alex was also chosen by the readers of *Quilter's Newsletter* magazine (February 2009) as "The Most Influential Person in The Quilting Industry" (in a three-way tie with Ricky Tims and Karey Bresenhan of Quilts, Inc.).

Alex's personal mission is not only to share her love of quilting with anyone who will listen, but also to educate and encourage those interested in quilting, as clearly and simply as possible, so quilting can continue to be handed down from generation to generation.

Alex has two children and lives in Northern California with her husband.

**alexandersonquilts.com
thequiltshow.com**